Contents

Language Arts

Phonics/Initial Consonants 2
Phonics—Vowels, Short Vowels 3–4
Long Vowel Puzzle 5
Word Identification 6
Initial Consonants 7
Sentence Comprehension 9
Alphabetical Order 15
Rhyming Words 16
Verbs 17
Antonyms 18
Safety Awareness 19
Compound Words 22
Story Order 28, 52
Vowels/Sea Animals 29
Rhyming Words/Transportation 32
Reading Comprehension 34–35
Following Directions/Story Order 41
Week Days/Reading a Calendar 42
Alphabetical Order/Counting 45
Sentences—Naming Part/ Independence Day 53
Reading an Invitation 54
Sentences—Telling Part 55
Contractions 56
Sentences—Naming Part 62
Adjectives 63
Capitalization/Community Workers 64
Positional Prepositions 65
Reading Comprehension/ Story Order/Plants 67
Verb Forms 72
Punctuation and Capitalization 73

Social Studies

Map Skills/ Reading Comprehension 20–21, 24–25

Math

Number Recognition/Problem Solving 10
Ordinal Numbers 11
Missing Addends/Adding 12
Counting Money 13, 23, 61
Coin Values/Addition 14
Patterns 26
Geometric Shapes/Number Words 33
Interpreting a Picture Graph/ Counting by Twos 36
Estimation 37
Sums and Differences 44
Addition and Subtraction Facts/ Number Code 46–47
Addition and Subtraction 48
Graphing/More and Fewer 49
Place Value 50
Skip Counting by Fives and Tens 51
Telling Time: Hour 57
Interpreting a Graph/ More and Fewer 58–59
Telling Time: Half Hour 60
Fractions 66
Geometric Shapes/Counting 68
Logic/Chart Skills 69
Coordinates 70–71

Science

Seasons 8
Classification/Living and Non-Living 27
Landform Recognition 30
Climate Recognition 31
Insect Identification 38
Animal Life Cycles 39
Observing Nature 40
Weather/Interpreting a Picture Graph 43

And More...

Activities to Share 74–75
Answer Key 76–80

Puzzling Names

Write the first letter of each picture's name.
Read the animal names.
Write the problem numbers in the boxes by the correct animals.

1. ____ ____ ____ ____

2. ____ ____ ____ ____ ____ ____

3. ____ ____ ____ ____ ____

Try This!

Make a puzzle! You need: nature magazines to cut up, scissors, glue, and heavy paper or cardboard.

1. Cut out a large picture of an animal.
2. Glue the picture onto cardboard or heavy paper.
3. Cut the picture into puzzle pieces.
4. Put your puzzle back together.

Water World

The letters **a**, **e**, **i**, **o**, and **u** are **vowels**.

A **long vowel** says its own name.
Color the long vowel fish **orange**.

A **short vowel** makes a different sound.
Color the short vowel fish **green**.

Help the squid get to her cave.
Draw a line to connect the long vowel fish.

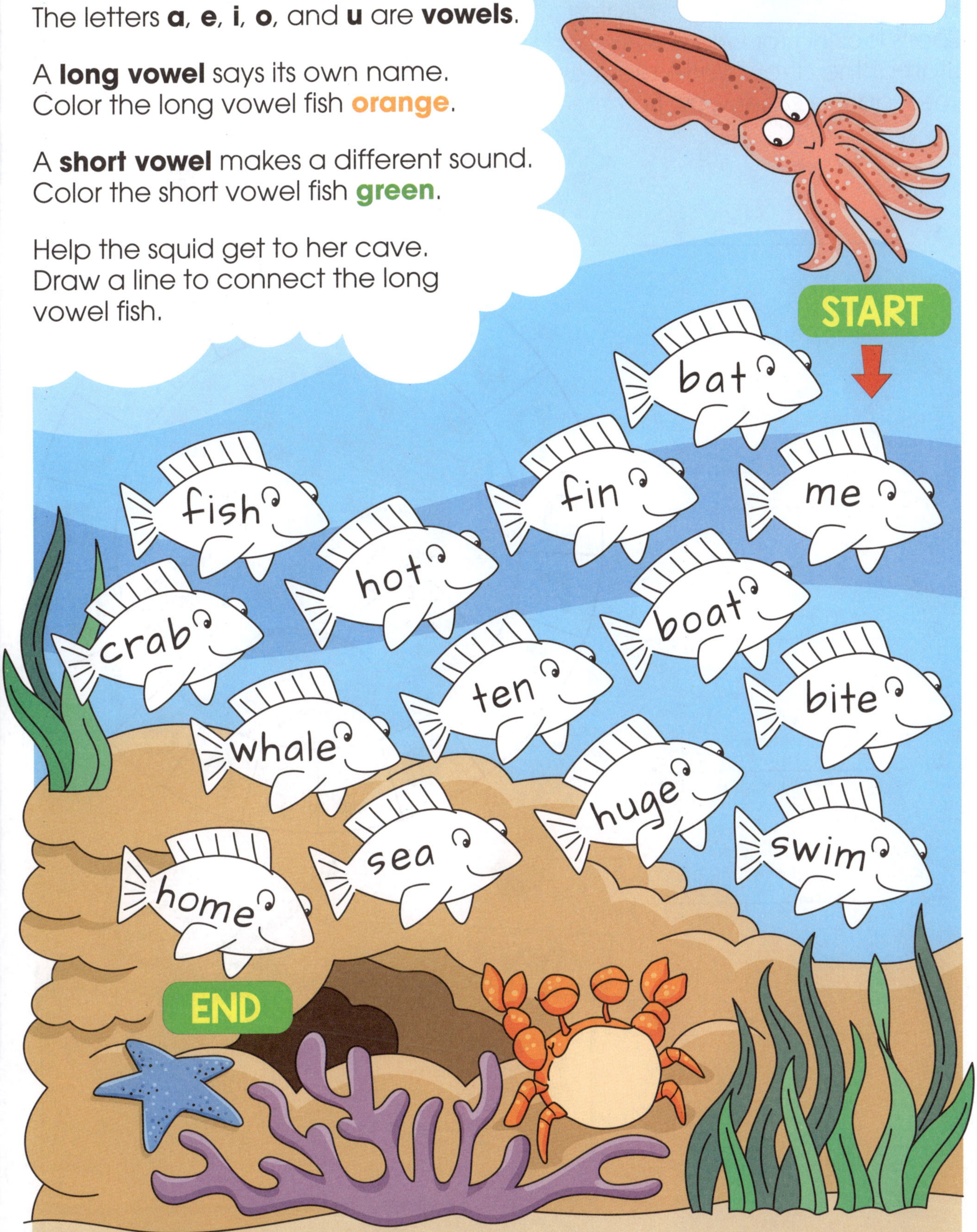

Honey Bear

Honey Bear is running in circles!
She is looking for words with short vowel sounds.
Start at the arrow. Write eight words you find.
Then go the other way. Say the words.

1. ____________________

2. ____________________

3. ____________________

4. ____________________

5. ____________________

6. ____________________

7. ____________________

8. ____________________

Try This!

Have an adult help you make this honey of a treat.

2 apples, cored & peeled	½ cup walnut pieces
½ cup raisins	¼ cup apple juice
1 tablespoon honey	8 graham crackers

1. Chop the apples, walnuts, and raisins.
2. Stir in the juice and honey.
3. Spread on crackers. Eat!

Puzzling Vowels

As you've learned, the letters **a**, **e**, **i**, **o**, and **u** are **vowels**.
A **long vowel** sounds like its name.
These words have **long vowel** sounds:

c**a**ke

tr**ee**

h**i**ve

r**o**pe

m**u**le

Look at the pictures. Say the words.
Write the long vowel in the puzzle.

ACROSS

1. 

4. 

6. 

DOWN

2. 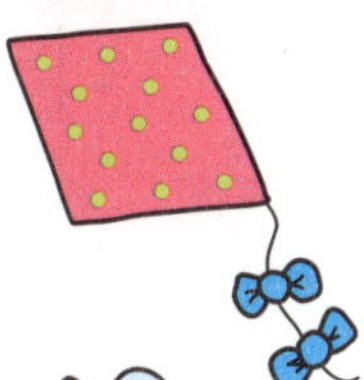

3. 

5. 

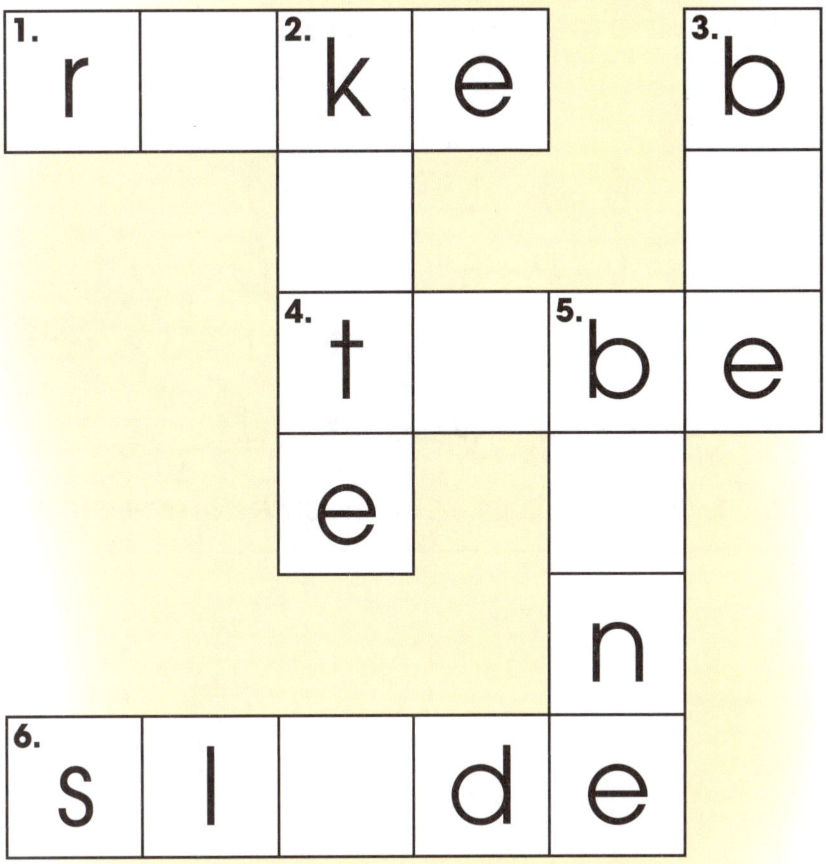

Summer Fun

Dani and Josh live on Shady Lane.
Three friends live there, too.

School is out! Summer fun begins!
Circle the friends' names in the puzzle.

S T W E N W
B I L L Y T
L P E D R O
K C D A N I
G J O S H J

HOT IDEA

Make a word puzzle using the names of friends. Ask one friend to solve the puzzle.

Draw a picture of your favorite summertime activity.

Follow the Friends!

What does each friend like to do in the summer?
Write a letter from the box to finish each word.

b h s c f r

_____ wim

_____ amp

_____ ish

_____ ide

_____ ike

_____ aseball

What do you like to do?

____

HOT IDEA

Think of things you can do with a group of friends. Try to put on a magic show, go stargazing, plant a garden, or have a garage sale.

Here Comes Summer!

What things go with summer?
Draw a line from each summery picture to the sun.

beach towel

beach ball

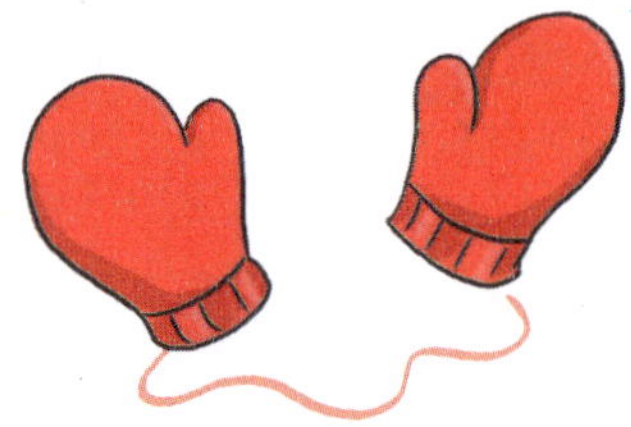
mittens

shorts

boots

suitcase

watermelon

baseball cap

picnic basket

HOT IDEA

Write a summer poem:
Bright, hot sun.
Campers having fun.
Swimmers on the go.
NO cold snow!

snowman

swimsuit

Baseball Fever

It is time for baseball practice. Dani and Josh run outside.
Read the sentences. Write each friend's name by his or her house.

Dani and Josh

Billy has a flower garden. His house is blue.

Pedro has a pond. His house is red.

Wen has a fence. Her house is yellow.

Giggles

Josh: Mom, may I go out and play?
Mom: With those holes in your socks?
Josh: No, with Billy, Pedro, and Wen!

Go Team!

The five friends play for the Rockets. Write each child's number on his or her shirt.

Dani is number **six**.
Josh is number **one**.
Pedro is number **three**.
Billy is number **eight**.
Wen is number **seven**.

There are 9 players on a baseball team.
How many more players are needed to play a game? ________

COOL FACT

The Baseball Hall of Fame is in Cooperstown, New York.

Batter Up!

Read what each friend says.
Write their names in order.

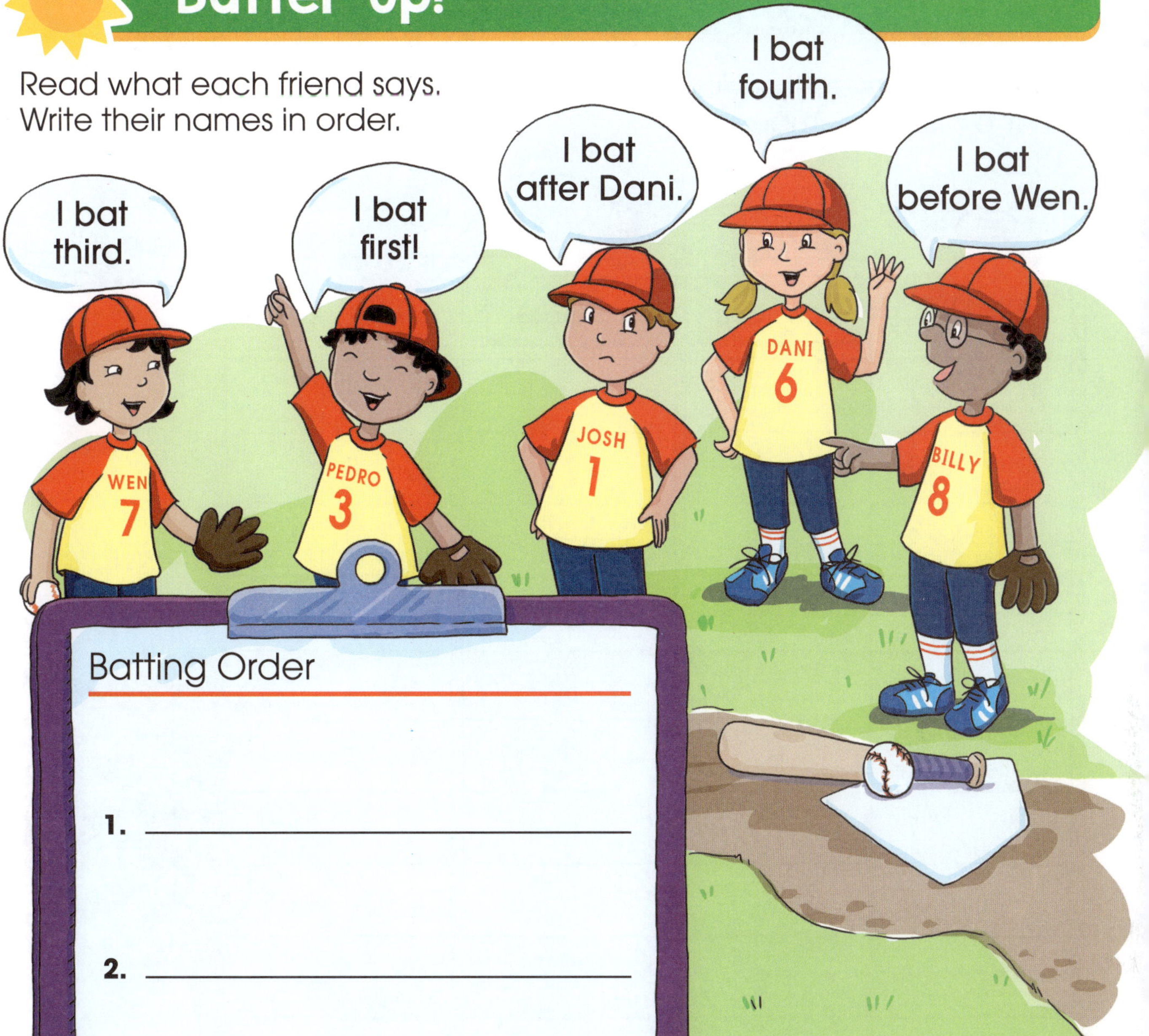

Batting Order

1. ______________________________

2. ______________________________

3. ______________________________

4. ______________________________

5. ______________________________

Keeping Score

The Rockets played their first game with the Flyers.
Fill in the missing numbers.

Giggles

What makes a baseball stadium stay cool?

The fans!

INNING	Rockets	Flyers	TOTAL RUNS
1	1		3
2		2	4
3	1		1
4		0	2
5		3	5
6	1		2
7			
8			
9			
TOTAL			17

How many innings did they play? ________

Who won the game? ______________________________

Team Treat!

After the game, the Rockets were hungry.
Circle the coins needed to buy each item with exact change.

Quarter = 25¢ Dime = 10¢ Nickel = 5¢ Penny = 1¢

1.

2.

3.

4.

Making Cents

Write the price of each item. Then add and write the total.

1.

____

\+ ________

How much for both? ________

2.

____

\+ ________

How much for both? ________

3.

____

\+ ________

How much for both? ________

4.

____

\+ ________

How much for both? ________

Splash City

The water park opens today! From 1–6, number the names in alphabetical order.

Welcome to Splash City!

☐ Slippery Slide

☐ Paddleboats

☐ Wave Pool

☐ Log Ride

☐ Tube Trails

☐ Beach

Which would be your favorite ride?

____

HOT IDEA

Play a game of water volleyball. Use a water balloon instead of a ball.

Slippery Slide Ride

Help Wen get down the waterslide. Circle the word pairs that rhyme. Then draw a line to connect the rhyming word pairs.

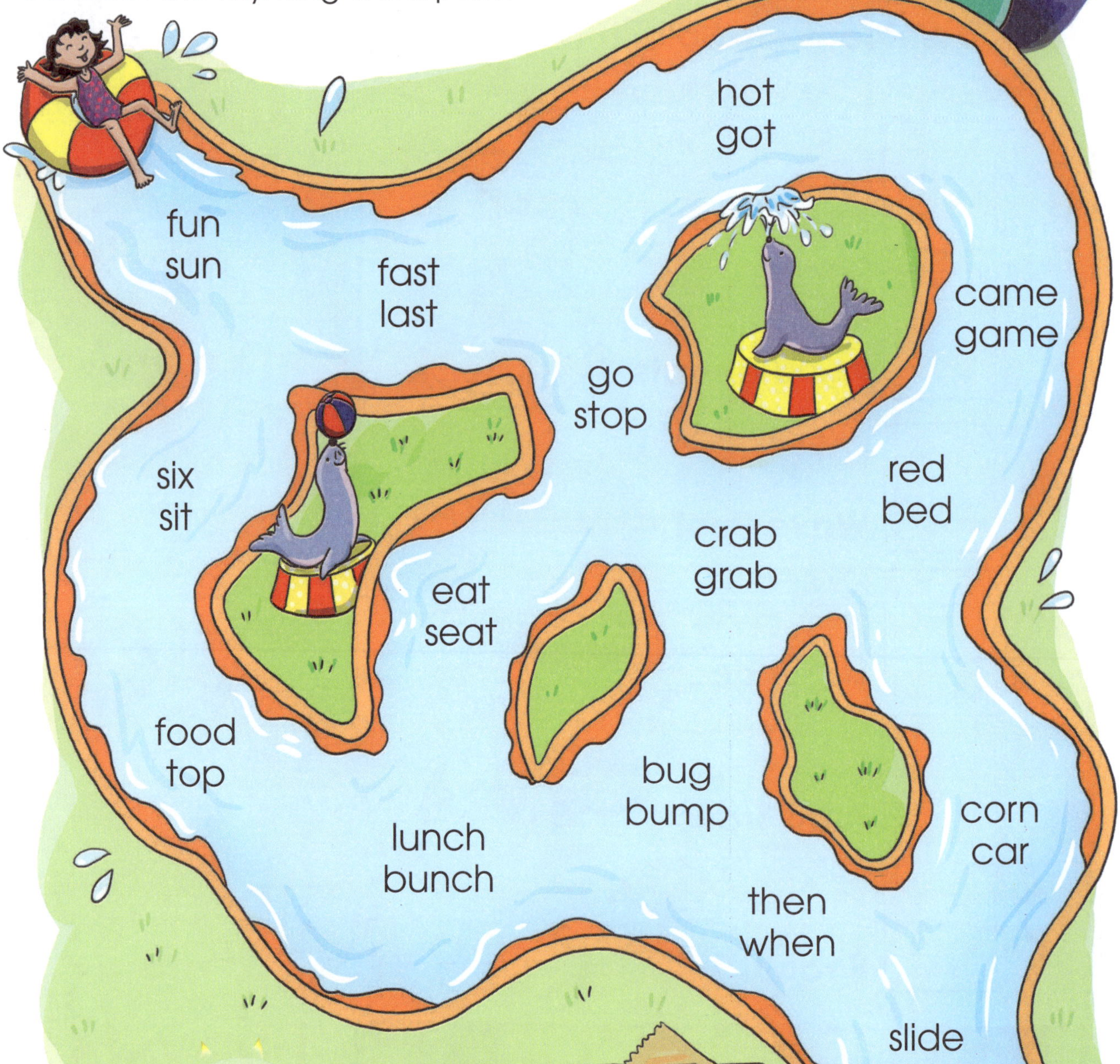

HOT IDEA

Make a waterslide. With your parents' help, lay a plastic sheet about 10–15 feet long on the grass. Set your water sprinkler so it "rains" on the plastic sheet. Take a running start and slide on your stomach.

Play Like the Animals!

Action words tell what people and animals do.
Under each picture, write an action word from the box.
Then draw lines to match the children with the animals doing the same actions.

climb dig slide jump

1. ______________________ 2. ______________________

3. ______________________ 4. ______________________

Ride the Waves!

Read each word in the wave pool.

Write a word from the pool that means the opposite.

1. out ______________
2. warm ______________
3. little ______________
4. quiet ______________
5. slow ______________
6. sad ______________

Try This!

Try making frozen bubbles. Blow a few bubbles onto a plate, and put the plate in the freezer. What happens?

Draw yourself in the pool with a friend.

That's Not Right!

Look at the wave pool. What's not right?
Circle up to 9 things that don't look right.

Write one pool rule.

HOT IDEA

You don't want to get too much sun on a hot summer day. Make a sun hat for yourself. You will need: a piece of newspaper (two pages with a fold down the middle).

1. Fold the outer edges down to make a point at the top center.
2. Fold the bottom flap up to meet the bottom of the triangle.
3. Then fold it over again.
4. Do the same on the other side.

Off to the Dude Ranch

Pedro and his family are spending a week at Circle S Ranch. Answer the questions to help them get to the riding stables.

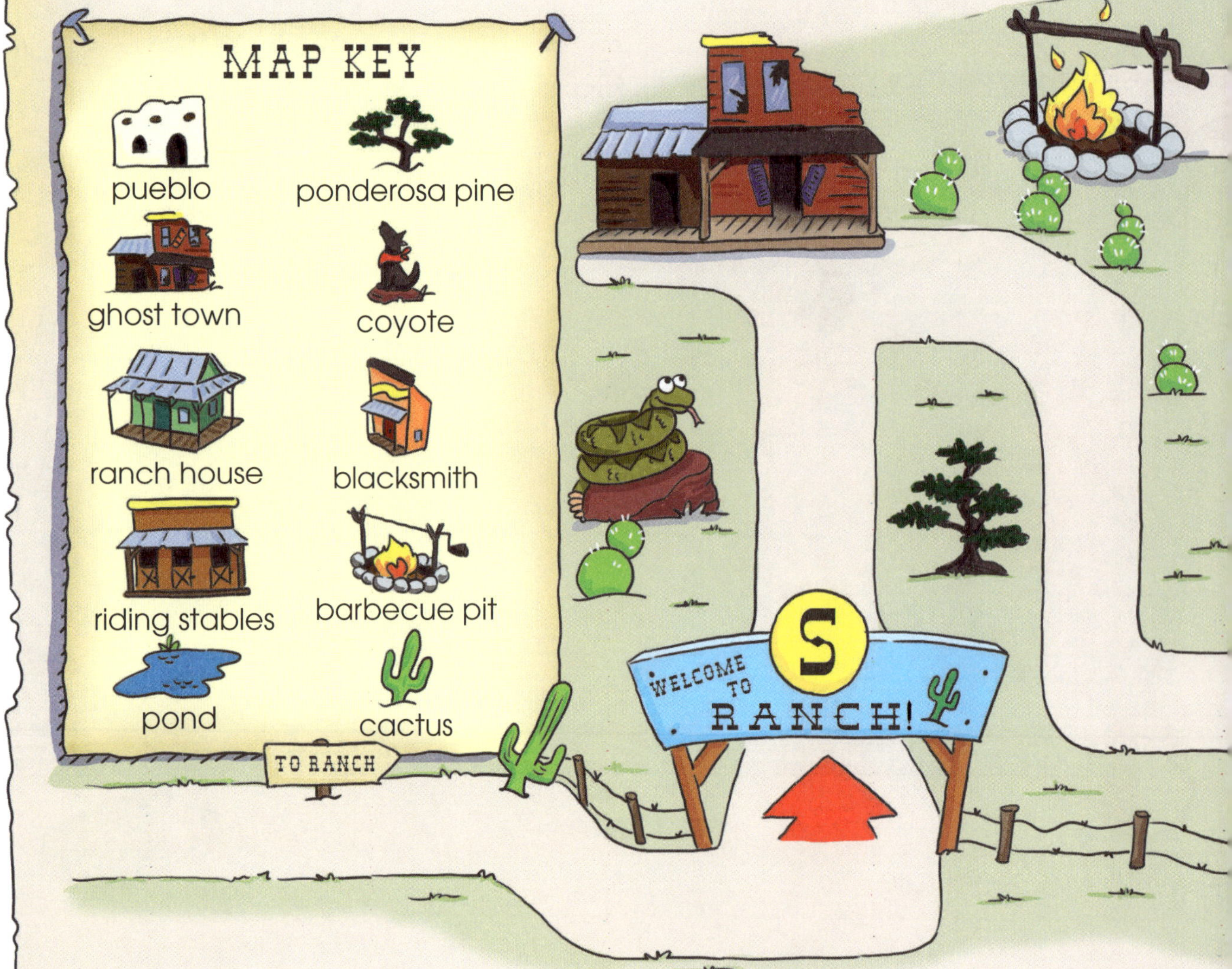

1.	What will they pass first?	ghost town	cows
2.	Will they turn at the ranch house?	yes	no
3.	Will they cross over a bridge?	yes	no
4.	What will they pass after the bridge?	coyote	pueblo
5.	What is the last thing they will pass?	barbecue pit	pond

Draw a line to show the path.

Which two things would you like to see at Circle S Ranch?

____

____

COOL FACT

There are hundreds of ghost towns across the United States. Do you know of any ghost towns near where you live?

Giddyup!

Draw lines between horses that make compound words.

HOT IDEA

Whether you are riding or walking the trail, make a nutty mix to take along for a snack. Mix together some bite-size crackers, dried fruits, mixed nuts, cereal, and chocolate chips. YUM!

Saving for Souvenirs

Josh and Dani saved money for a family trip.
Count the money each one has.
Write the amounts on the lines.

Josh

Quarters

_____ ¢

Dimes

_____ ¢

Nickels

_____ ¢

Pennies

_____ ¢

Josh's Total: _____ ¢

Dani

Quarters

_____ ¢

Dimes

_____ ¢

Nickels

_____ ¢

Pennies

_____ ¢

Dani's Total: _____ ¢

HOT IDEA

To make a great souvenir of your summer travels, take along a cap and a permanent marker. Ask new friends you meet along the way to sign your cap.

Who saved more?

____

Camping Out!

Dani and Josh went on a family camping trip. Use the map to answer the questions.

1. Is there a camper by the playground? yes no
2. Is there a path to the lake? yes no
3. Is the hiking trail near the camp store? yes no

HOT IDEA

With your parents' help, warm marshmallows over a fire. Eat them between two graham crackers with a piece of chocolate. YUM!

4. Are tents and campers in the same area?	yes	no
5. Is the picnic area near the tree fort?	yes	no
6. Is there a bathhouse by the lake?	yes	no

Summer at the Seashore

Wen's family took a trip to the beach.
Name the beach things Wen sees.
Color the pictures to continue the patterns.

Draw and color the pictures to continue the patterns.

Giggles

Knock, knock!
Who's there?
Shell.
Shell Who?
She'll be coming 'round the mountain when she comes!

On the Beach

Wen and her family saw many things at the beach. Write the name of each thing in the correct column of the chart.

COOL FACT

Hermit crabs don't make their own shells. They find a shell that fits and move in. If they don't, they might be eaten by a gull!

Living Things	Non-Living Things

Dig In!

Wen and her brother like to build sandcastles.
Write 1, 2, 3, 4, 5 to show the order in which things happened.

Giggles

Why is the beach so noisy?

Because waves are always breaking on it!

As a Matter of Fact

vowel code:
a e i o u
● ▲ ★ ◆ ■

Read each animal fact. Use the vowel code to write each animal's name. Write each sentence's number in the box next to the animal it describes.

1. I have eight arms and large eyes.

◆ c t ◆ p ■ s ______________________

2. I blow myself up when I am scared.

b l ◆ w f ★ s h ______________________

3. I have a soft body, so I find a shell to live in.

h ▲ r m ★ t c r ● b ______________________

4. I have sharp teeth on my snout.

s ● w f ★ s h ______________________

5. I talk with whistles, chirps, and other sounds.

d ◆ l p h ★ n ______________________

Travel Tips

Billy's family is planning a trip. They read about different places.
Write the missing word to complete each book's title.
Use the words in the box.

Island	Mountain	Desert	Forest

SPEND THE NIGHT

in the Coyote

____________________!

Camping Is Great

in Black Bear

____________________!

TURTLE

____

A Great Place to Visit!

CLIMB

Giant

____________________!

Different Places

Fill in the missing word to complete each sentence. Use the words in the box.

water	**dry**
cold	**hot**
trees	

1. It's very ____________ high in the mountains.

2. Some deserts are ____________ during the day.

3. The sand is ____________ from a lack of rain.

4. Islands are surrounded by ____________ .

5. Forests are lands with ____________ .

Where does Billy's family go?
Unscramble the letters, and write the words:

t o y o e C   e s D r t e

____

Giggles

How is an island like the letter t?

Both are in the middle of water.

Getting There

Summer is a good time to travel. People go from place to place across the country. What different kinds of transportation do they use?

Read each rhyme. Then write the type of transportation each rhyme describes.

1. I rhyme with hike. ____________________

2. I rhyme with us. ____________________

3. I rhyme with star. ____________________

4. I rhyme with pet. ____________________

5. I rhyme with plane. ____________________

Travel Shapes

Follow the directions to draw a jet and a ship.

1. Draw an oval.
2. Add five triangles.
3. Draw squares for windows. Add some clouds.

Where would you like a jet to take you?

____

1. Draw 5 rectangles.
2. Add two triangles.
3. Draw ten circles. Add some waves.

Where would you like a ship to take you?

____

Wish You Were Here!

Read each postcard. Draw lines to match the cards with the friends who wrote them. Write the name(s) on each card.

Hi,
We are having a great time camping. We saw deer and a bear yesterday. Wish you were here.

____

____

Howdy,
This ranch is lots of fun. I ride a horse named Sugarlump. I learned to rope a calf. There is a cookout tonight.

____

Write words from the box to answer the questions.

ocean	calf	bear	horse	desert

1. Dani and Josh saw what animal? ______________________

2. Where did Wen swim? ______________________

Hi,
The desert is neat. One cactus is taller than my house! I heard a coyote last night. See you soon.

____

Hi,
The ocean is great!
I swim every day.
I have made three sandcastles. Wish you were here to look for seashells with me.

____

HOT IDEA

If you could build a bridge from your house to anywhere in the world, where would it be? Why?

3. What animal did Pedro rope? ______________________

4. Who is Sugarlump? ______________________

5. Where does a cactus grow? ______________________

Gone Fishing

The five friends are home from their trips. They went fishing. Read the picture graph. Write the number of fish each one caught.

Circle the correct answers.

1. Who caught the most fish?

2. Who caught the fewest fish?

3. Who caught the same number of fish?

Giggles

What's the difference between a piano and a fish?

You can tune a piano, but you can't tuna fish!

Fish Tales

Dad's fish is 4 pennies long.

Estimate how many pennies long each fish is.
Now measure with pennies.
How close were your guesses?

Estimate	Measurement

COOL FACT

When a fish called a flounder hatches, it has one eye on each side of its head. After living on the bottom of the sea, one eye twists around so that both eyes are on one side of the flounder's head.

Nature Spy

Josh and Wen are looking for insects. Not all bugs are insects.

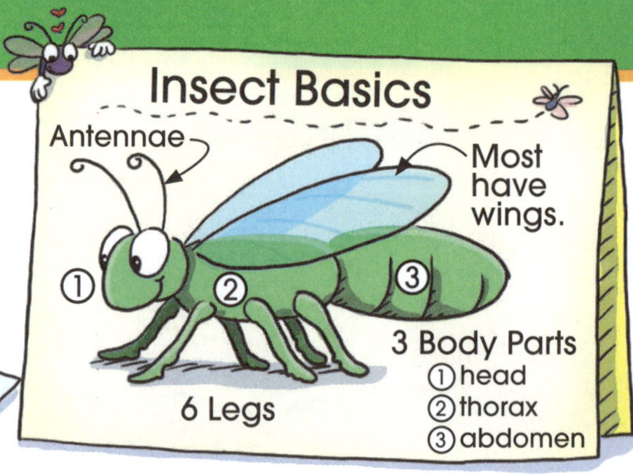

Check the boxes next to the bugs that are insects.

COOL FACT

A click beetle has a special talent. If it is on its back, it will slowly bend in the middle and pop straight up into the air with a loud "click!"

Froggy Grows Up

Look at the pictures.

A B C D E

Read the sentences.
Write **A**, **B**, **C**, **D**, and **E** to show how Froggy grows up.

1. ________ Froggy is a tiny tadpole.

2. ________ Froggy is a big frog.

3. ________ Froggy is an egg.

4. ________ Froggy grows four legs.

5. ________ Froggy grows two legs.

Buggy Backyard

Josh and Wen decided to be detectives for the day.
Look at the picture.
Circle the hidden insects.

How many insects did you find?

Go outside. Look at an insect with a magnifying glass.
Draw what you see.

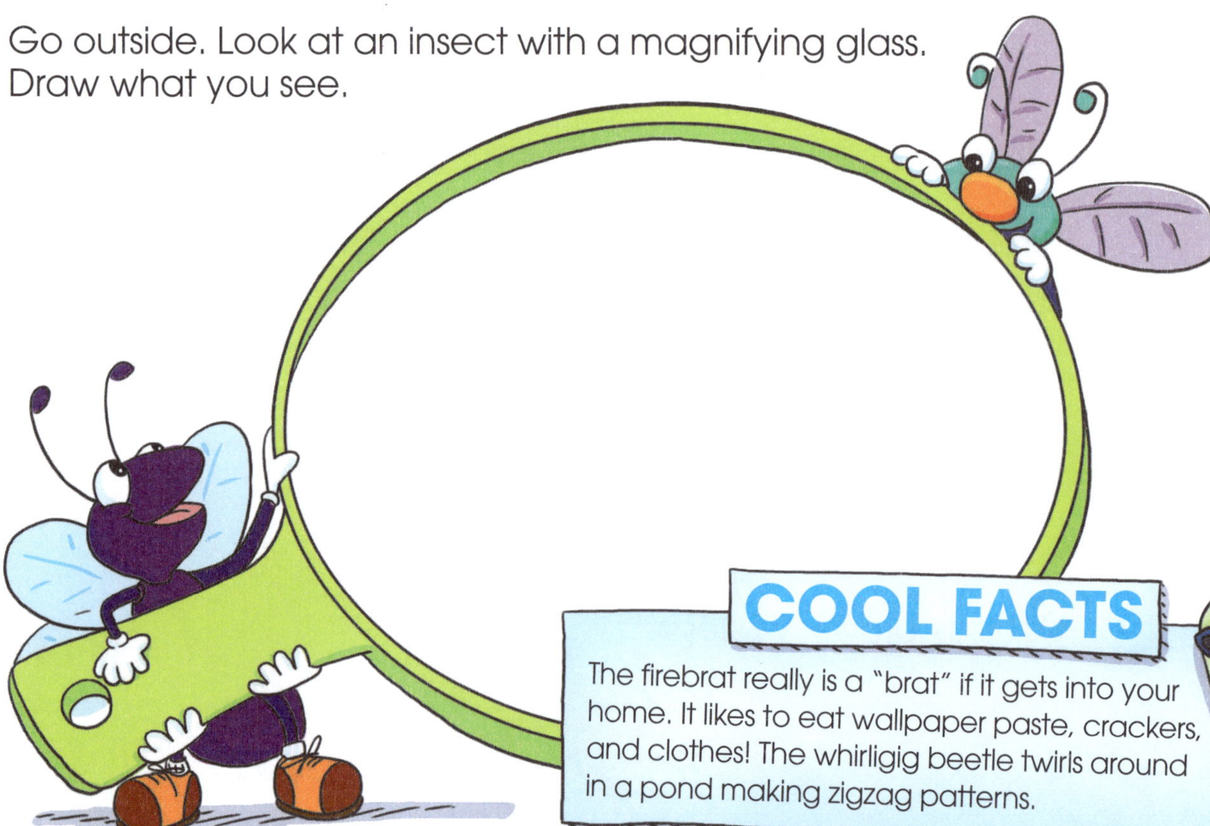

COOL FACTS

The firebrat really is a "brat" if it gets into your home. It likes to eat wallpaper paste, crackers, and clothes! The whirligig beetle twirls around in a pond making zigzag patterns.

Rub-a-Dub-Dub

Josh and Dani planned a neighborhood dog wash.
Read the sentences. Draw a line to show where they go.

1. They go to Mrs. Green's house first.
2. They go to Mr. Berry's house next.
3. Then they go to the Ride house.
4. They go to Mrs. Ball's house last.

HOT IDEA

Write a rhyme about washing a dog. Use rhyming words such as rub, dub, tub, and scrub.

Rub-a-dub-dub,
Washing dogs in a tub.
Rub-a-dub-dub,
How many dogs did they scrub?

What's Happening?

This calendar tells what is happening where the friends live.

Sunday	Monday	Tuesday	Wednesday	Thursday	Friday	Saturday
Berry picking at Eno Farm	Farmers' Market Opens Today!	Berry Baking Contest	4th of July Parade at 11:00	Fireworks at the Lake at 9:00	County Fair Today through Saturday	Blue Ribbon Day at the Fair

Write the days when these things happen.

1.  ______________________

2.  ______________________

3.  ______________________

4.  ______________________

June Weather

This is a picture graph about the weather in June.

1. On how many days did people need an  ? ________

Why? ____

2. On how many days would you wear  ? ________

Why? ____

3. What kind of weather happened least during June?

____

Bonus!

What month comes after June? ____________________

Farmers' Market

Write each sum. Color the picture.

1. 8 + 3 = ______

2. 11 – 3 = ______

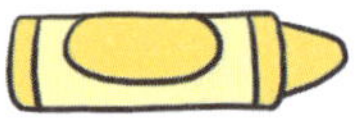

3. 6 + 6 = ______

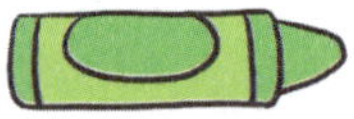

4. 12 – 6 = ______

5. 5 + 4 = ______

6. 9 – 4 = ______

HOT IDEA

Make math flash cards you can solve and eat!
Spread peanut butter on graham crackers.
Use licorice whips to form a number problem.
Solve the problem and eat!

One Potato, Two Potatoes

Write the food names in alphabetical order.
Count how many there are. Write the numbers.

Foods in Alphabetical Order	Amount

HOT IDEA

Count the fruits and vegetables again. This time, count backwards!
3 - 2 - 1 melons!

Sheep Shearing Today!

Write a number sentence about each picture.

1. ______ + ______ = ______ **2.** ______ − ______ = ______

3. ______ + ______ = ______ **4.** ______ − ______ = ______

5. ______ + ______ = ______ **6.** ______ − ______ = ______

Who Is Hiding?

One animal with hooves is very shy.
He is hiding behind these numbers.
Find the **sums** and **differences** of the numbers in each column.
Then use the code to find out the animal's name.

7	8	9	10	11	12	13	14	15
r	e	s	m	t	o	f	s	v

5	12	8	5	10
+8	−6	+2	+7	−3
−7	+3	−5	−6	+7
+4	+3	+7	+8	−6

Look at the last number in each column. Write the correct letters from the code box to spell the animal's name.

______ ______ ______ ______ ______

Desert Trail

Follow the path through the desert.
Add numerals to write the **sums**.
Subtract numerals to write the **differences**.

Graph It!

Fill in the graph. Color one box for each fruit and vegetable on page 45.

Giggles

What is it called when apples come tumbling off of the counter at the market?

An apple-lanche!

Type of Food

Type of Food								
apples								
bananas								
carrots								
lettuce								
melons								
potatoes								
Amount	**1**	**2**	**3**	**4**	**5**	**6**	**7**	**8**

Circle the correct answers.

1. Are there more apples or potatoes?
2. Are there more melons or heads of lettuce?
3. Are there fewer carrots or bananas?
4. Are there fewer apples or carrots?

How Many?

The friends saw many kinds of fruits and vegetables.
Count how many there are. Write the numbers.

1. _______ tens _______ ones

How many? _______

2. _______ tens _______ ones

How many? _______

3. _______ tens _______ ones

How many? _______

4. _______ tens _______ ones

How many? _______

5. _______ tens _______ ones

How many? _______

6. _______ tens _______ ones

How many? _______

How many tens are there? How many ones are there?

	tens	ones
40		
36		

Bunches of Berries

Billy and Pedro went berry picking.
Pedro made piles of 5 berries. Count by fives.
Write the numbers. The first one is done for you.

5 ____ ____ ____ ____

____ ____ ____ ____ ____

How many berries did Pedro pick? ☐

Billy made piles of 10 berries. Count by tens.
Write the numbers. The first one is done for you.

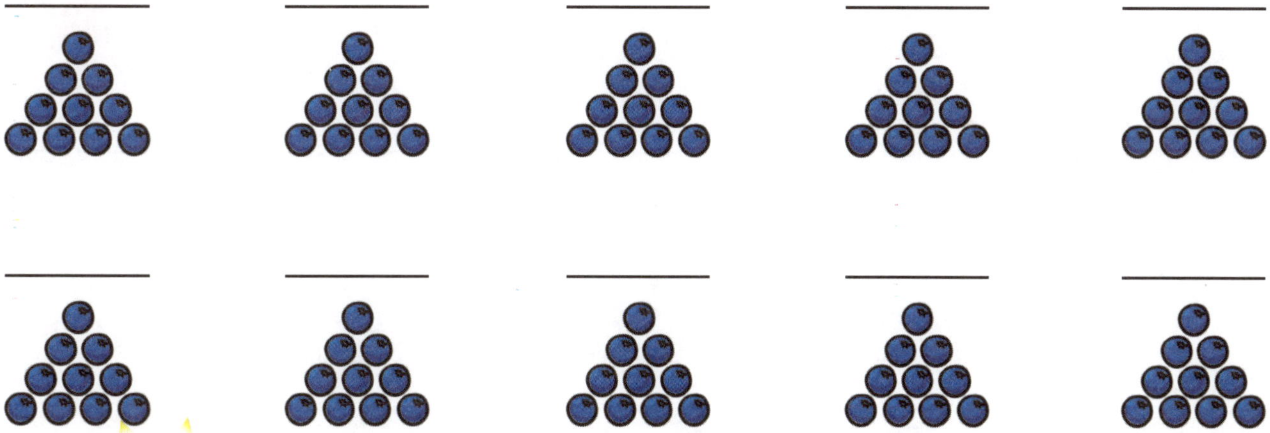

10 ____ ____ ____ ____

____ ____ ____ ____ ____

How many berries did Billy pick? ☐

HOT IDEA

Juicy Painting

Mash blueberries through a sieve. Use the juice to paint a picture. What color is the juice?

Berry Good Muffins

Billy and Pedro made blueberry muffins for their friends.
Write 1, 2, 3, 4 to show the order in which things happened.

Bake until golden brown.

Mix the batter first.

Add blueberries to the mixed batter.

Pour the batter into muffin cups.

HOT IDEA

Make your own Blueberry Muffins! *Parent-Supervised Activity

You need:

$1\frac{3}{4}$ cups flour	$\frac{1}{2}$ tsp. salt	2 eggs
$\frac{1}{3}$ cup sugar	$\frac{1}{4}$ cup cooking oil	1 tsp. vanilla
2 tsp. baking powder	$\frac{3}{4}$ cup milk	1 cup blueberries

1. Heat oven to 400°. Put 12 paper baking cups in a muffin tin.
2. Combine the dry ingredients.
3. Mix the oil, milk, eggs, and vanilla together. Add wet mixture to dry ingredients.
4. Stir in berries.
5. Pour the batter into muffin cups.
6. Bake 20–25 minutes or until golden brown. YUM!

Hooray for the Red, White, and Blue!

Each year on July 4, we celebrate our country's birthday. This day is called Independence Day. It began in 1776.

A sentence has a **naming part**.
The naming part tells who or what the sentence is about.
Write the naming part of each sentence.
The first one is done for you.

1. The parade begins at 2:00 p.m. ____parade____

2. Pedro will carry the flag. ____________

3. Drums will be played. ____________

4. Bells will ring. ____________

5. Our town loves a parade. ____________

Party Time!

Read the invitation.

COME TO A PARTY!

What:	4th of July Picnic
When:	July 4 at 2:00 p.m.
Where:	123 Shady Lane
Who:	Wen Chu

Bring your favorite picnic food.

Circle the correct answers.

1.	Who is having a party?	Billy	Wen
2.	What is the party for?	4th of July	Wen's birthday
3.	What day is the party?	June 5	July 4
4.	What time is the party?	2:00 p.m.	12:00 p.m.
5.	Where will the party be?	123 Shady Lane	Billy's house

What picnic food would you bring to the party?

____

____

____

____

Giggles

Where can a burger get a great night's sleep?

On a bed of lettuce!

Backyard Barbecue

A sentence has a **telling part**.
The telling part tells what someone or something does.

Underline the telling part of each sentence.
The first one is done for you.

1. Dani brings milk.
2. Josh has bananas.
3. Wen takes a salad.
4. Billy carries hot dogs.
5. They all eat together.

Write a sentence about a picnic.
Underline the telling part.

____

Bonus! Who didn't bring anything? ____________________

Kaboom!

What are the friends saying about the fireworks? Use words from the box to write each contraction.

Isn't	Don't	We're	Let's	I'm

HOT IDEA

Make a Fourth of July Spinner!

You need: string, scissors, crepe paper, and a spring clothespin.

1. Cut a piece of string as long as your arm.
2. Thread the string through the hole in the clothespin and tie a knot.
3. Cut crepe paper strips as tall as you.
4. Clip the clothespin to one end of the strips.
5. Hold the end of the string and wave your arm to twirl the strips.

County Fair Fun

Write the time next to each clock.
Draw lines to match the clocks to what happens at those times.

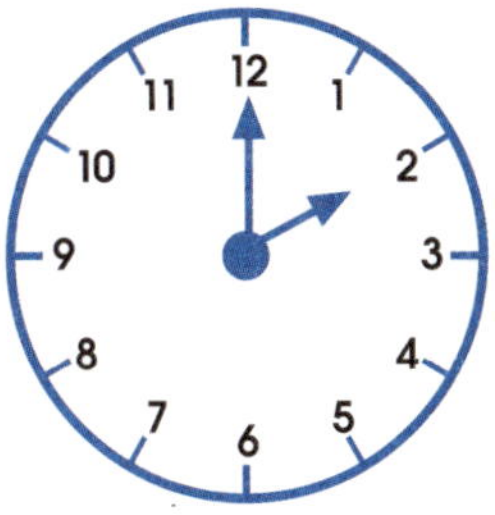

1. _____ o'clock

2. _____ o'clock

3. _____ o'clock

4. _____ o'clock

5. _____ o'clock

Events at the Fair

Use the graph to answer the questions.

How many people were at each event?
Write the correct number in each box.

Pie Contest   Tractor Pull   Horse Show   Flower Show

Which event had the **fewest** people?

Which event had the **most** people?

Blue-Ribbon Pie

Use the graph to answer the questions.

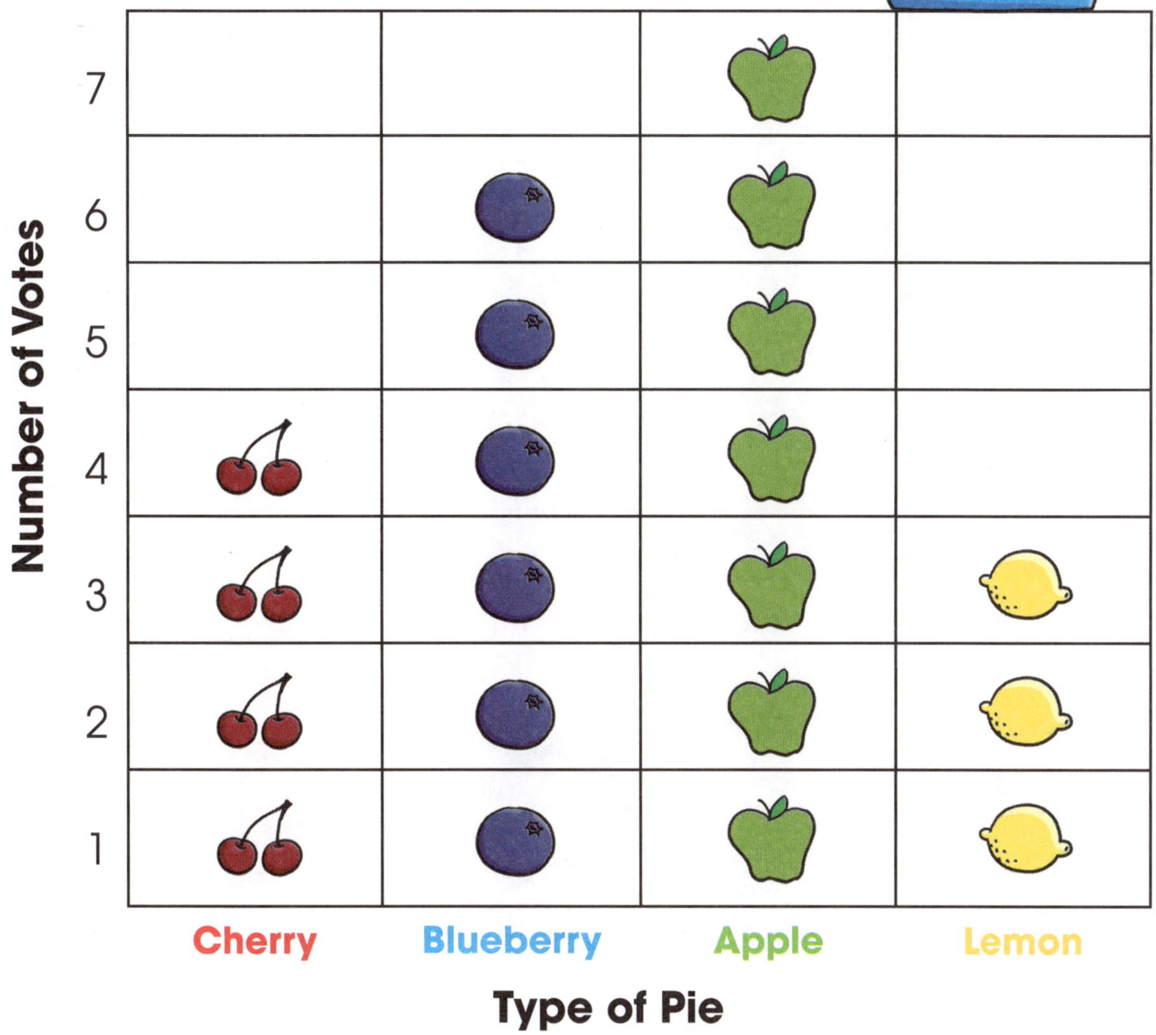

How many people like each type of pie?
Write the correct number in each box.

Cherry Pie   Blueberry Pie   Apple Pie   Lemon Pie

Which kind of pie was the favorite? Circle the favorite pie.

What a Ride!

Write the time below each clock.

1. 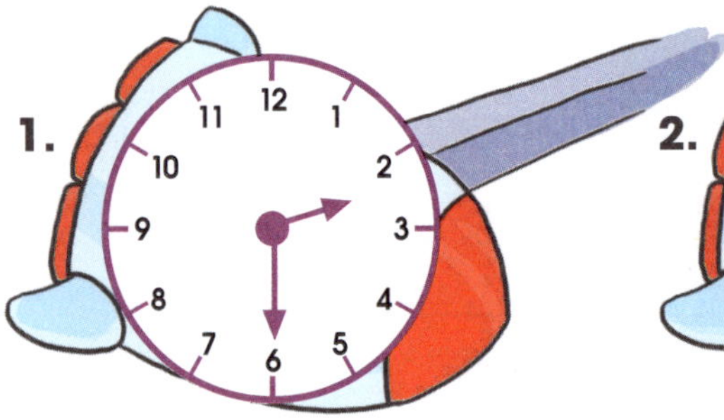

half past ____

____ : ____

2. 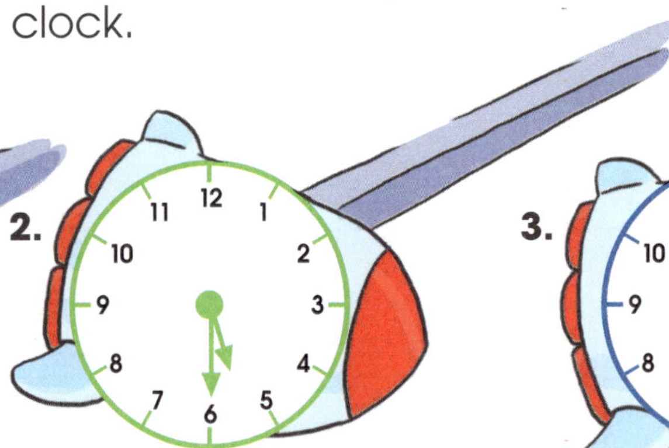

half past ____

____ : ____

3. 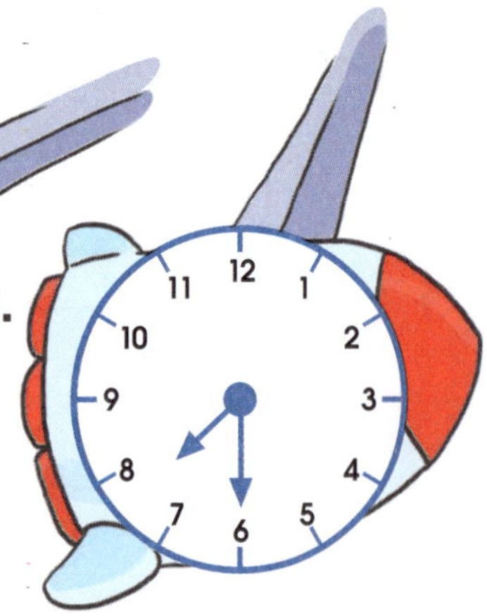

half past ____

____ : ____

Draw hands on each clock to show each time.

How Much?

Fill in how many coins Billy needs to make each amount. The first one is done for you.

	Quarter	Dime	Nickel	Penny
8¢	0	0	1	3
15¢				
20¢				
46¢				
39¢				
58¢				

HOT IDEA Set up a "pretend" auction with your friends. Collect items that will go up for bid. You be the first auctioneer and have your friends make bids on an object. The highest bidder counts out the correct amount of "play money" to pay. The highest bidder then becomes auctioneer, and the bidding begins on a new item.

Animals at the Fair

Fill in the missing naming word to complete each sentence. Use the words in the box.

pig	horse
dog	duck
cow	goat

1. The ____________ is tall.
2. The ____________ is fat!
3. The ____________ has horns.
4. The spotted ____________ moos.
5. The ____________ eats corn.
6. Is the ____________ lost?

Describe It!

Giggles

Why don't baby leopards like to play hide-and-seek?

Because they are always spotted!

Describing words tell about naming words.

The **huge** lion roared.

Which word tells about, or **describes**, the lion?
Some describing words tell how animals look or feel.

Write words that tell about the animals.

1

2

3

long tall tiny wet sleepy huge

6

4

5

1. ______________________ **2.** ______________________

3. ______________________ **4.** ______________________

5. ______________________ **6.** ______________________

We Work at the Zoo!

Here are four people who work at Zippity Zoo.
Circle the name in each sentence.

Remember—A person's name begins with a capital letter.

Jan helps sick animals.

Bob keeps animal homes clean.

Chan teaches sea animals.

Lisa feeds hungry animals.

Write the correct name under each picture.

1. ______________________

2. ______________________

3. ______________________

4. ______________________

Try This!

To make dough names, you need: 1 cup peanut butter, 1 cup honey, and 2 cups powdered milk.

1. Wash your hands.
2. Mix the ingredients in a bowl.
3. Add more milk if the dough is too sticky.
4. Form the dough into the letters of your name.
5. Eat your name!

Where Are the Animals?

Where are the animals on the Desert Trail?
Finish each sentence with a word from the box.
The first one is done for you.

over under in across on

1. The roadrunner  runs under the .

2. The lizard  sleeps ______________ the .

3. The jackrabbit  leaps ______________ the .

4. The snake  glides ______________ the .

5. The owl  sits ______________ the .

Try This!

Play a game of Simon Says with family members or friends. Use the words from the word box on this page as you play.

My, My, What a Pie!

Circle the correct pizzas.

1. Billy and Pedro get an equal share.
How did they cut the pizza?

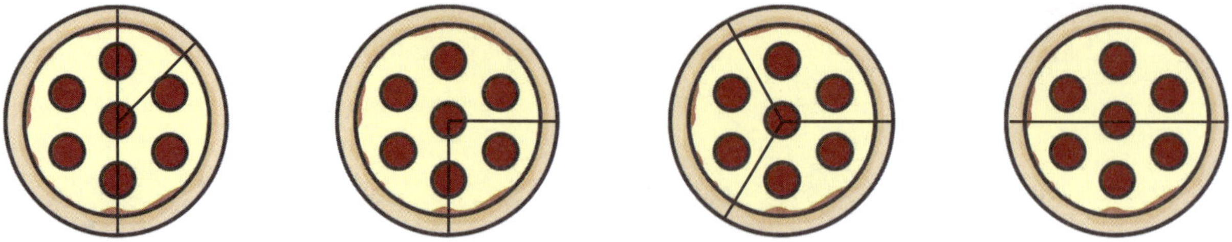

2. Dani, Josh, and Wen get an equal share.
How did they cut the pizza?

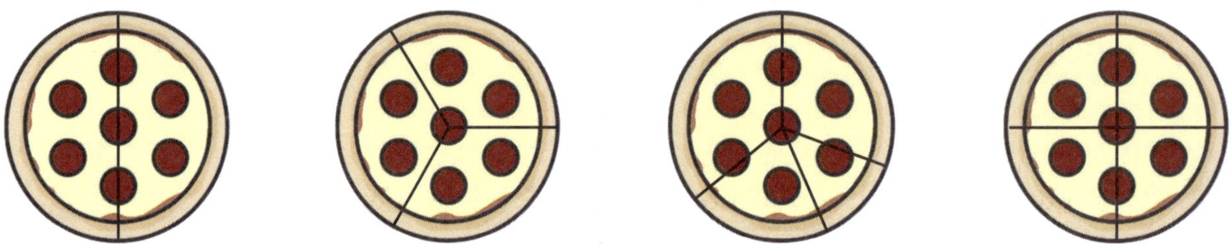

3. Billy, Dani, Wen, and Josh get an equal share.
How did they cut the pizza?

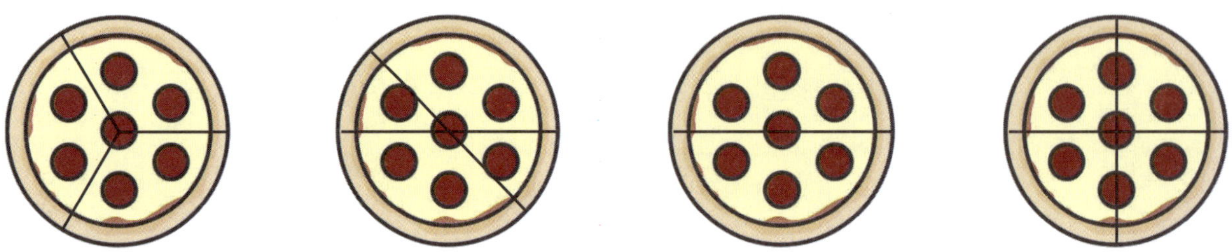

4. Circle the picture that shows $\frac{2}{3}$ of the apples colored.

Growing, Growing, Grown

Josh grew a watermelon. In the spring, he planted seeds. He watered his plant each day. The sun made it grow. By summer, the watermelon was huge! He brought it to the fair. He won a blue ribbon!

Circle the correct answers.

1. Who is the story about?

   Dani   Josh   Pedro

2. What fruit was grown?

   apples   watermelon   bananas

3. What did the plants need?

   water, rain, clouds   soil, sun, plants   soil, water, sun

4. Write 1, 2, 3, 4 to show the order in which things happened.

COOL FACT

In Arizona, the saguaro cactus can grow to be more than 50 feet tall.

Crafty Winners

Look at the front of each birdhouse. Write how many sides, corners, and square corners you can see for each.

1.

_______ sides

_______ corners

_______ square corners

2.

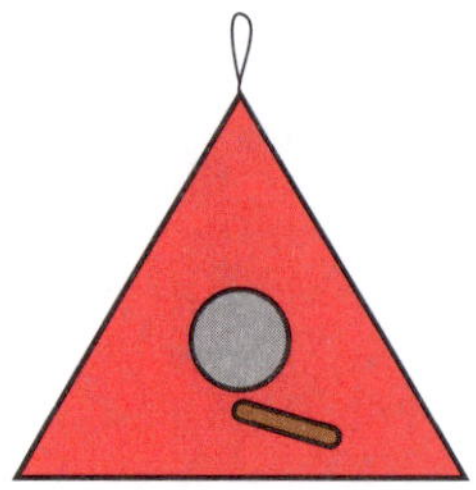

_______ sides

_______ corners

_______ square corners

3.

_______ sides

_______ corners

_______ square corners

4.

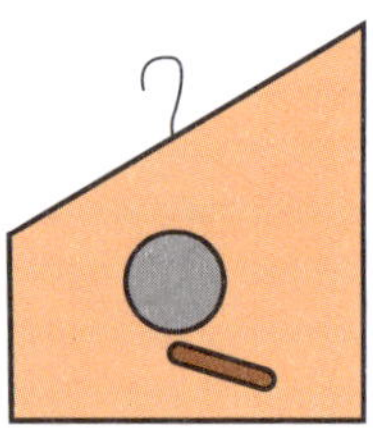

_______ sides

_______ corners

_______ square corners

5.

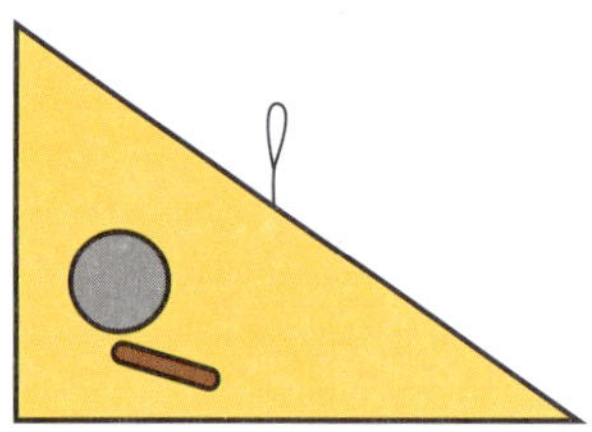

_______ sides

_______ corners

_______ square corner

6.

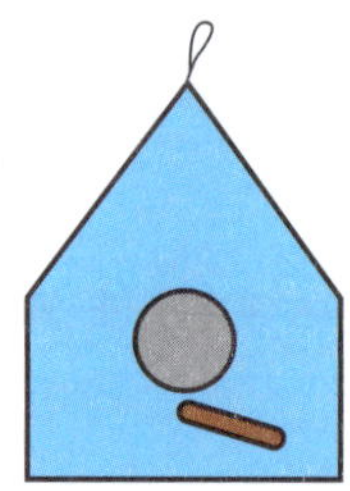

_______ sides

_______ corners

_______ square corners

Giggles

When you do not eat much, it is said that you eat like me. But I am always eating, when I'm not nesting in a tree. Who am I?

A bird.

Critter's Cafe

Read the clues. Mark the chart with ✓s.
The first one is done for you.

1. Everyone had fruit.
2. Dad and Ben had a taco.
3. Mom had a salad.
4. Anna had a turkey sandwich.
5. Mom, Ben, and Anna had juice.
6. Dad had milk.

	milk	juice	fruit	salad	taco	sandwich
Dad			✓			
Ben			✓			
Mom			✓			
Anna			✓			

Write the correct person's name under each meal.

1. ______________________

2. ______________________

3. ______________________

4. ______________________

Try This!

Make critter place mats. You need: construction paper, crayons or pens, and clear contact paper. Draw animals on the construction paper. Cover the construction paper with clear contact paper.

Cool Stuff for School

Summer is over. School will start soon.
The friends are doing some back to school shopping.

Use the grid on page 71 to see where each thing is found.
Write the aisle and row where each item is located.
The first one is done for you.

1. Find the . Aisle 3 Row 3

2. Find the . Aisle ______ Row ______

3. Find the . Aisle ______ Row ______

4. Find the . Aisle ______ Row ______

5. Find the 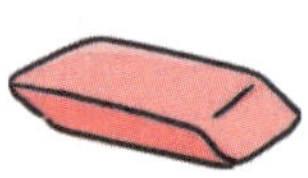. Aisle ______ Row ______

6. Find the . Aisle ______ Row ______

7. Find the 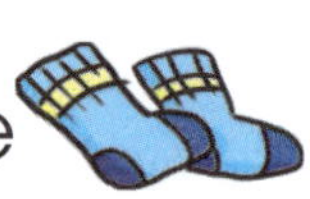. Aisle ______ Row ______

8. Find the . Aisle ______ Row ______

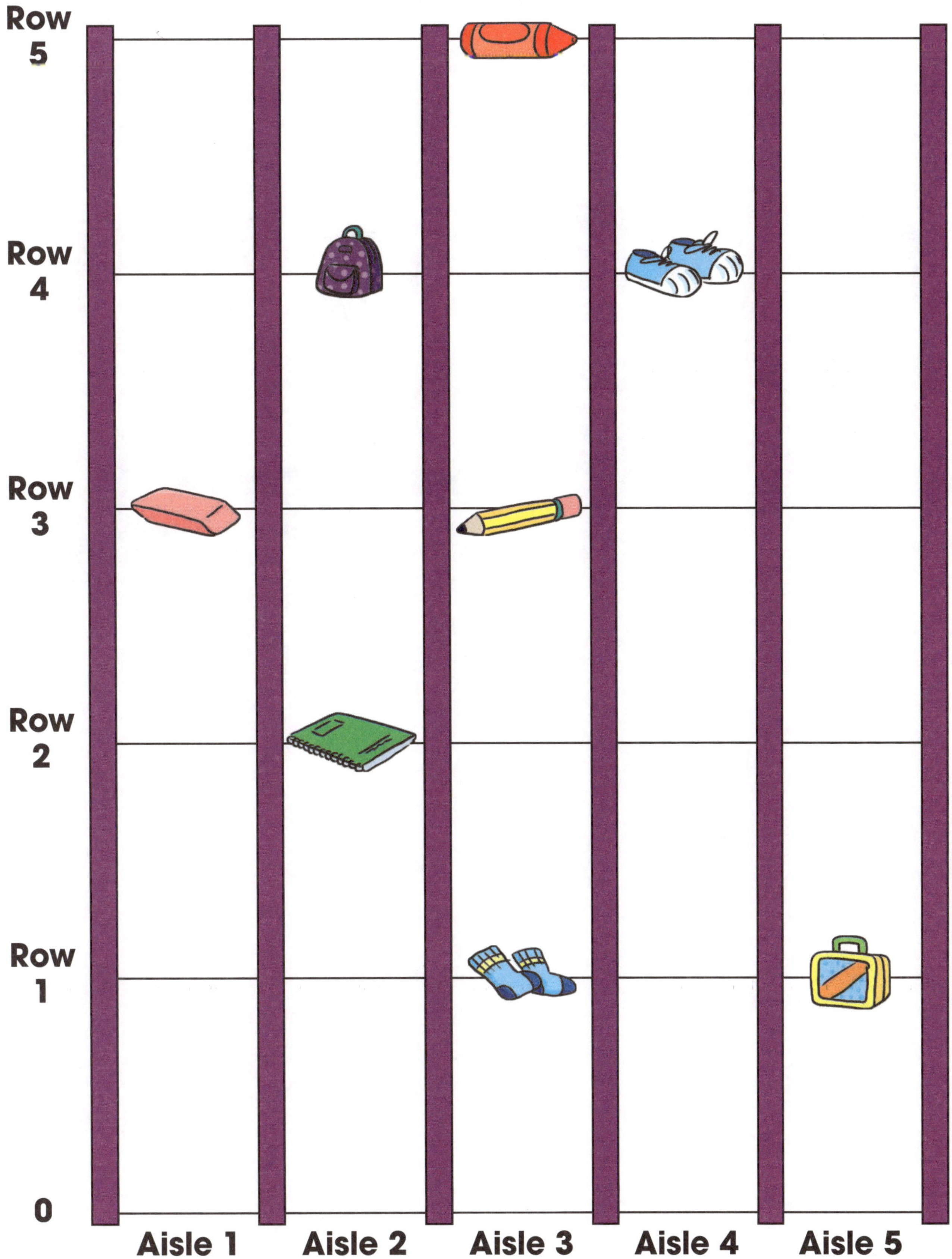
Row 5
Row 4
Row 3
Row 2
Row 1
0
Aisle 1
Aisle 2
Aisle 3
Aisle 4
Aisle 5

Back to School

Use was to tell about one.
Use were to tell about more than one.

Fill in the missing verb to complete each sentence.

1. The friends ____________________ ready for school.
2. Dani ____________________ walking to school.
3. Pedro ____________________ waiting for Billy.
4. Wen and Josh ____________________ talking on the bus.
5. They ____________________ all happy to be back in school.

Next Summer

Use a period (.) to end a sentence that tells.
Use a question mark (?) to end a sentence that asks.
Use this mark ≡ to show where a capital letter goes.

Correct the sentences below by adding the proper marks. The first one is done for you.

1. did you have a nice summer?

2. name one thing you did

3. will you take a trip next summer

4. do you know where you will go

5. i hope you have lots of fun

6. Write a sentence about what you did this summer.

____

____

Activities to Share

Language Arts

Treasure Hunt

Organize a treasure hunt in your home or outside. Following a list of simple directions to find the hidden treasure will give your child a fun way to practice reading.

Write a Story!

Help your child staple sheets of blank paper together. Ask your child to make up a story. Have your child tell who the story is about and what will happen to that character. Encourage your child to illustrate the story once the words are written in the book. Read the story to your child, and have your child read the story to you.

Be sure to check out the Words Are Categorical Series. These entertaining books make learning the different parts of speech fun and interesting. Titles in the series include the following:

Dearly, Nearly, Insincerely: What Is an Adverb? by Brian P. Cleary, illustrated by Brian Gable. Lerner Publishing Group, 2003.

Hairy, Scary, Ordinary: What Is an Adjective? by Brian P. Cleary, illustrated by Jenya Prosmitsky. Carolrhoda Books, 2001.

I and You and Don't Forget Who: What Is a Pronoun? by Brian P. Cleary, illustrated by Brian Gable. First Avenue Editions, 2006.

A Mink, a Fink, a Skating Rink: What Is a Noun? by Brian P. Cleary, illustrated by Jenya Prosmitsky. Lerner Publications Company, 1999.

Pitch and Throw, Grasp and Know: What Is a Synonym? by Brian P. Cleary, illustrated by Brian Gable. First Avenue Editions, 2007.

To Root, to Toot, to Parachute: What Is a Verb? by Brian P. Cleary, illustrated by Jenya Prosmitsky. Carolrhoda Books, 2001.

Stop and Go, Yes and No: What Is an Antonym? by Brian P. Cleary, illustrated by Brian Gable. First Avenue Editions, 2008.

Social Studies

Keeping a Travel Journal

When you travel, encourage your child to keep a travel journal to record place names, points of interest, meals, accommodations, mileage, and so on. Postcards, photos, and other documentation can be taped or glued into the journal.

A Day at the Beach

Cool breezes, the smell of fresh salt air, the feel of sand between your toes—it's all at the beach! If you are planning a trip to the beach, here are a few tips for your family about what to bring. Make a list of things to bring, including sunscreen, sunglasses, towels, hats, pails, things to dig with, big T-shirts to wear for exploring, a sweatshirt if the air turns cool once the sun goes down, and mesh bags for shell collecting.

Check out this and other Social Studies books at your local library or bookstore:

Geography from A to Z: A Picture Glossary by Jack Knowlton, illustrated by Harriet Barton. HarperCollins, 1997. Learn about important geographical terms in this interesting reference book. Each entry has a clear description and bright illustration.

Science

High Tide, Low Tide

If you and your family like to look for treasures on the beach, the best beachcombing happens right after the tide goes out during low tide. This is when you are likely to find treasures that the high tide left behind. Look on the weather page of your local newspaper for the time of the next tide.

A Seashore Zoo

It's okay to collect sea creatures to observe, as long as you return them to their habitat. First, make a habitat for them, such as a pail or see-through container into which you have put sand, rocks, seaweed, and a container of seawater. Observe your sea creature for awhile, and then return it to the sand and sea. Draw a picture and write notes about what you observe.

Check out these and other Science books at your local library or bookstore:

How Many Ways Can You Catch a Fly? by Robin Page, illustrated by Steve Jenkins. Houghton Mifflin, 2008. Learn about the different ways that animals solve challenges like finding food, building shelters, and staying out of danger. The book features amazing facts and vibrant illustrations.

Science Detectives: How Scientists Solved Six Real-Life Mysteries by the Editors of YES Mag, illustrated by Rose Cowles. Kids Can Press, 2006. Learn how scientists put their detective skills to work to solve mind-boggling mysteries. The book features plenty of facts and stories, as well as five projects that provide opportunities for hands-on involvement in testing science-detection skills.

Math

Rainbow Snack

Measuring is a good way to practice fractions. Measure and mix these ingredients for a tasty snack.

- 1 cup of fruit-flavored puffed cereal
- 1 cup of fruit-flavored cereal shaped like Os
- $\frac{1}{2}$ cup of sunflower seeds
- $\frac{1}{2}$ cup of peanuts or mixed nuts
- $\frac{1}{2}$ cup of raisins and other dried fruits

Put all of the ingredients into a small plastic bag. Give the bag a good shake. Your snack is ready for travel!

Check out these and other Math books at your local library or bookstore:

Fraction Fun by David A. Adler, illustrated by Nancy Tobin. Holiday House, 1997. This book provides a lively introduction to fractions. Coins are studied, and the fractional value of each coin is determined. Plus, readers are sure to agree that pizza is a delicious way to learn about numerators and denominators!

You Can't Buy a Dinosaur with a Dime by Harriet Ziefert, illustrated by Amanda Haley. Blue Apple Books, 2007. This humorous story tells about how Pete saves his allowance, spends too much, and starts over. The rhyming story allows readers to compute with Pete as he saves and spends.

Answer Key

Page 2

1. swan
2. bobcat
3. zebra

Page 3

Page 4

clockwise: fast, stop, top, pat, ten, tent, tub, bat, at, trap, rap, pot;
counterclockwise: fat, top, par, part, art, tab, but, net, tap, pot, pots

Page 5

1. r	a	2. k	e		3. b
		i			e
		4. t	u	5. b	e
		e		o	
				n	
6. s	l	i	d	e	

Page 6

S	T	(W	E	N)	W
(B	I	L	L	Y)	T
L	(P	E	D	R	O)
K	C	(D	A	N	I)
G	(J	O	S	H)	J

Pictures will vary.

Page 7

swim
camp
fish
ride
hike
baseball
Favorite activities will vary.

Page 8

Summer things:

beach ball
beach towel
watermelon
baseball cap
shorts
suitcase
picnic basket
swimsuit

Page 9

Names by houses in clockwise order:

Pedro
Billy
Wen

Page 10

To play a game, the Rockets need 4 more players and another team of 9 players to play against. So, 13 total players are needed.

Page 11

1. Pedro
2. Billy
3. Wen
4. Dani
5. Josh

Page 12

INNING	Rockets	Flyers	TOTAL RUNS
1	1	2	3
2	2	2	4
3	1	0	1
4	2	0	2
5	2	3	5
6	1	1	2
7			
8			
9			
TOTAL	9	8	17

6 innings
The Rockets

Page 13

1. 

2. 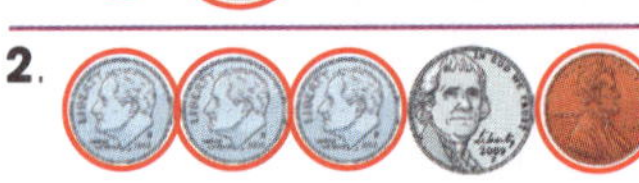

3. 

4. 

Answer Key

Page 14

1. 20¢ + 75¢ = 95¢
2. 44¢ + 50¢ = 94¢
3. 42¢ + 34¢ = 76¢
4. 35¢ + 52¢ = 87¢

Page 15

4 Slippery Slide
3 Paddleboats
6 Wave Pool
2 Log Ride
5 Tube Trails
1 Beach
Favorite rides will vary.

Page 16

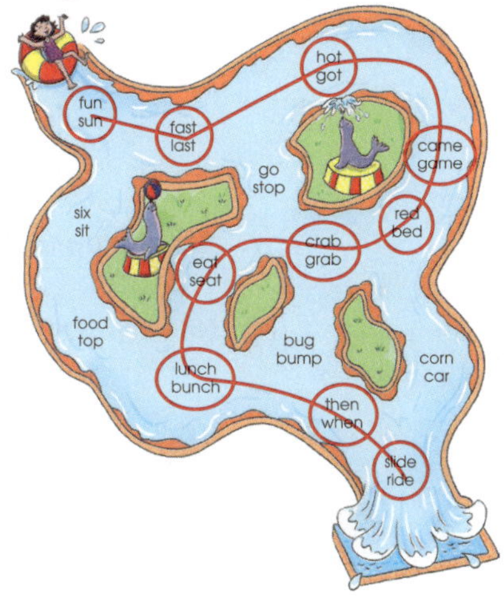

Page 17

Page 18

1. in
2. cool
3. big
4. loud
5. fast
6. happy

Drawings will vary.

Page 19

Rules will vary.

Pages 20-21

1. ghost town
2. no
3. yes
4. coyote
5. pond

Things to see will vary.

Page 22

Page 23

Josh	Dani
50¢	50¢
30¢	20¢
10¢	15¢
2¢	1¢
92¢	86¢

Josh has saved more money.

Pages 24-25

1. yes
2. yes
3. no
4. no
5. yes
6. yes

Answer Key

Page 26

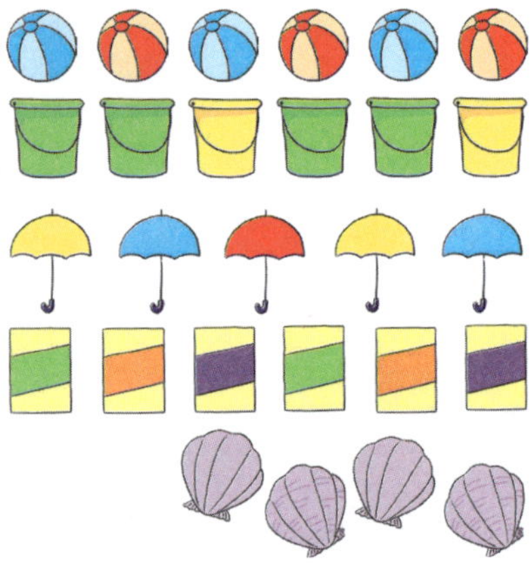

(colored red ball)

(colored yellow pail)

(drew blue umbrella)

(drew yellow towel with orange stripe)

(drew shell with purple stripes)

Page 27

Living Things:
crab
lifeguard
seagulls
shells (Some shells are living.)

Non-Living Things:
boat
flag
kite
shells

Page 28

Page 29

1. octopus
2. blowfish
3. hermit crab
4. sawfish
5. dolphin

Page 30

Coyote Desert
Black Bear Forest
Turtle Island
Giant Mountain

Page 31

1. cold
2. hot
3. dry
4. water
5. trees

Billy's family is going to the Coyote Desert.

Page 32

1. bike
2. bus
3. car
4. jet
5. train

Page 33

Art and answers will vary. Look at the images to review your child's art.

Pages 34-35

1. bear
2. ocean
3. calf
4. horse
5. desert

Page 36

Number of fish:
6, 10, 6, 4, 8

Page 37

Length of fish (by pennies)
2
6
2
4
3
Estimations will vary, but they should be relatively close.

Page 38

Page 39

1. B
2. E
3. A
4. D
5. C

Answer Key

Page 40

There are 14 insects.
Insect drawings will vary.

Page 41

They washed 4 dogs.

Page 42

1. Thursday
2. Sunday
3. Wednesday
4. Saturday

Page 43

1. 7
Because it rained.
2. 10
Because it was sunny.
3. Cloudy days
Bonus: July

Page 44

1. 11
2. 8
3. 12
4. 6
5. 9
6. 5

Page 45

apples - 6
bananas - 7
carrots - 8
lettuce - 4
melons - 3
potatoes - 5

Page 46

1. 6 + 4 = 10 **2**. 9 − 4 = 5
3. 4 + 2 = 6 **4**. 8 − 3 = 5
5. 7 + 5 = 12 **6**. 7 − 2 = 5

Page 47

5 +8	12 −6	8 +2	5 +7	10 −3
13	6	10	12	7
−7	+3	−5	−6	+7
6	9	5	6	14
+4	+3	+7	+8	−6
10	12	12	14	8

moose

Page 48

Page 49

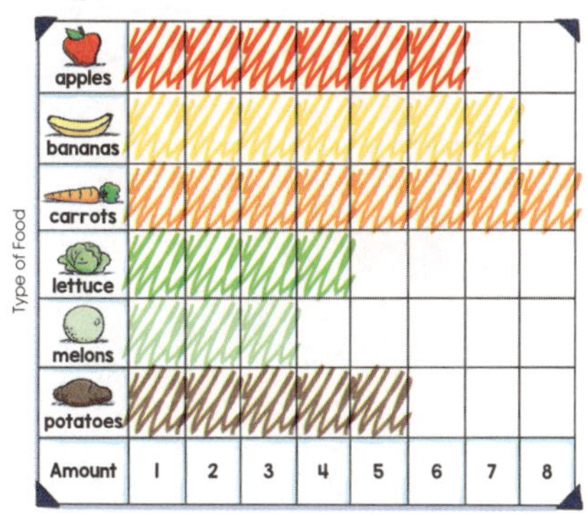

1. apples
2. lettuce
3. bananas
4. apples

Page 50

1. 3 tens 2 ones 32
2. 4 tens 0 ones 40
3. 3 tens 3 ones 33
4. 5 tens 3 ones 53
5. 3 tens 0 ones 30
6. 3 tens 6 ones 36

	tens	ones
40	4	0
36	3	6

Page 51

5, 10, 15, 20, 25,
30, 35, 40, 45, 50
Pedro picked 50 berries.
10, 20, 30, 40, 50,
60, 70, 80, 90, 100
Billy picked 100 berries.

Page 52

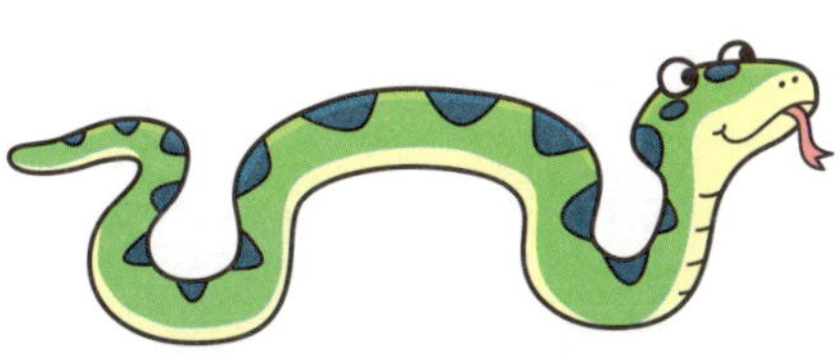

Answer Key

Page 53
1. parade
2. Pedro
3. Drums
4. Bells
5. town

Page 54
1. Wen
2. 4th of July
3. July 4
4. 2:00 p.m.
5. 123 Shady Lane

Foods will vary.

Page 55
1. brings milk
2. has bananas
3. takes a salad
4. carries hot dogs
5. eat together

Sentences will vary. Check to see that the telling part of the sentence is underlined.
Bonus: Pedro

Page 56
Let's watch!
Don't blink!
Isn't this great?
We're lucky!
I'm watching!

Page 57
1. 2 o'clock
2. 10 o'clock
3. 6 o'clock
4. 11 o'clock
5. 5 o'clock

Page 58
4, 6, 3, 5

 had the fewest.

 had the most.

Page 59
4, 6, 7, 3

 was the favorite pie.

Page 60
1. half past 2
   2:30
2. half past 5
   5:30
3. half past 7
   7:30

4.–7.

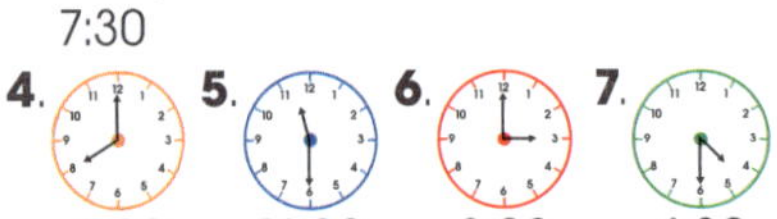

8:00 11:30 3:00 4:30

Page 61

	Quarter	Dime	Nickel	Penny
8¢	0	0	1	3
15¢	0	1	1	0
20¢	0	2	0	0
46¢	1	2	0	1
39¢	1	1	0	4
58¢	2	0	1	3

Other coin variations are acceptable.

Page 62
1. horse
2. pig
3. goat
4. cow
5. duck
6. dog

Page 63
1. wet 2. huge
3. tiny 4. sleepy
5. long 6. tall

Page 64
Circle Jan, Bob, Chan, and Lisa.
1. Bob 2. Jan 3. Lisa 4. Chan

Page 65
1. under 2. on 3. over
4. across 5. in

Page 66
1. 
2. 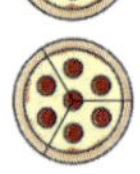
3. 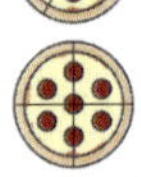
4. 

Page 67
1. Josh
2. watermelon
3. soil, water, sun
4. 

Page 68
1. 4, 4, 4
2. 3, 3, 0
3. 4, 4, 4
4. 4, 4, 2
5. 3, 3, 1
6. 5, 5, 2

Page 69
	milk	juice	fruit	salad	taco	sandwich
Dad	✓		✓		✓	
Ben		✓	✓		✓	
Mom		✓	✓	✓		
Anna		✓	✓			✓

1. Ben 2. Anna
3. Mom 4. Dad

Pages 70–71
1. Aisle 3, Row 3
2. Aisle 2, Row 2
3. Aisle 5, Row 1
4. Aisle 2, Row 4
5. Aisle 1, Row 3
6. Aisle 3, Row 5
7. Aisle 3, Row 1
8. Aisle 4, Row 4

Page 72
1. were
2. was
3. was
4. were
5. were

Page 73
1. did you have a nice summer?
2. name one thing you did.
3. will you take a trip next summer?
4. do you know where you will go?
5. i hope you have lots of fun.
6. Sentences will vary.

